What people are *

Resilience: Handlir
Time of C

This is a very thorough and useful resource for dealing with and managing one's anxiety during unforeseen circumstances, like the one we collectively find ourselves in now. George not only outlines how to recognize your anxiety, but also how to work with and ultimately transmute it so it becomes a tool for positive, personal growth. A book cannot of course replace the need for psychological or psychiatric care, but as a go-to resource to mitigate your own anxiety, you're in excellent hands.
Dr. Nicole Lipkin, Psy.D. MBA, CEO of Equilibria Leadership Consulting & Equilibria Psychological and Consultation Services and Founder, Young Leader Project

George Hofmann offers an honest, practical and refreshing look at the reality of anxiety in modern times. Reframing this everyday human experience in a way that undermines and challenges the destructive stigma that it carries. A heartfelt and thoughtful work that offers meaningful and realistic techniques for turning inward and engaging with all that troubles us.
Dave Smith, Mindfulness and Emotional Intelligence Trainer, Director of Programs, Secular Dharma Foundation

It might seem surprising that a clergyman is recommending a book that so often goes after belief. In talking about anxiety, George is calling us to question the beliefs that both occasion and are created by anxiety. (He does differentiate between these beliefs and faith!) He asks us to do the hard personal work of "sticking to the facts". Jesus promised that the truth will set us free. Jesus also said something about letting tomorrow worry for itself. If you struggle with anxiety, George's book provides some graceful and practical insights. We're all anxious some, but if yours has become debilitating, take care of yourself and seek the reality that can set you free of old story loops that are making you captive.

Michael Caine, Pastor-Teacher, Old First United Church of Christ

George Hofmann's book, *Handling Anxiety in a Time of Crisis*, is a primer for understanding and managing anxiety, negative thoughts, and social isolation. Focusing on movement, meditation, and meaningful work, his explanations are down-to-Earth, practical, and hopeful. George also takes the reader into his own life, candidly describing his struggles with anxiety, depression and bipolar disorder. His personal vulnerability is refreshing, easy to identify with, and comforting, reminding us that we're not alone in this all-too-human experience. As a clinical psychologist, I would recommend this book to anyone wrestling with the extra stresses caused by the coronavirus pandemic. You will find a good friend here with lots of good advice.

John C. Robinson, PhD., D. Min., author *Mystical Activism: Transforming a World in Crisis*

Resilience: Handling Anxiety in a Time of Crisis

The *Resilience* Series

Resilience: Handling Anxiety in a Time of Crisis

George Hofmann

CHANGEMAKERS
BOOKS

Winchester, UK
Washington, USA

JOHN HUNT PUBLISHING

First published by Changemakers Books, 2020
Changemakers Books is an imprint of John Hunt Publishing Ltd., No. 3 East Street,
Alresford, Hampshire SO24 9EE, UK
office@jhpbooks.com
www.johnhuntpublishing.com
www.changemakers-books.com

For distributor details and how to order please visit the 'Ordering' section on our website.

Text copyright: George Hofmann 2020

ISBN: 978 1 78904 679 3
978 1 78904 680 9 (ebook)
Library of Congress Control Number: 2020937315

A CIP catalogue record for this book is available from the British Library.

Design: Stuart Davies

UK: Printed and bound by CPI Group (UK) Ltd, Croydon, CR0 4YY
Printed in North America by CPI GPS partners

We operate a distinctive and ethical publishing philosophy in
all areas of our business, from our global network of authors to
production and worldwide distribution.

Contents

To Niki, for the inspiration and the opportunity to write.
Thanks and love always.

I would like to think of myself as being able to face whatever it is I have to face as me.
James Baldwin

Acknowledgments

Thank you to Tim Ward, Publisher of Changemakers Books, for the confidence, and John Hunt, Owner and Publishing Manager of the Resilience Series, John Hunt Publishing. To Benoit Dubé, MD for all you've done for me. To Brad and Valerie Krick; Jill Lipschutz Snyder; Ed Snyder; Rachel Margolin; Carlos Valdes-Dapena; and Nicole Lipkin for the input. Special thanks to Scott Vridalis and John Penn, and to my parents, in-laws and family. Love and dedication to Niki and Noelle. The quarantine goes on. We're pulling for each other.

Foreword

"What can we do to help?"

In a time of crisis - such as the 2020 Covid-19 pandemic - we all have a natural impulse to help our neighbors. John Hunt, founder of John Hunt Publishing, asked this question of our company, and then offered a suggestion. He proposed producing a series of short books written by experts offering practical, emotional, and spiritual skills to help people survive in the midst of a crisis.

To reach people when they need it most, John wanted to accomplish this in forty days. Bear in mind, the normal process of bringing a book from concept to market takes at least eighteen months. As publisher of the JHP imprint Changemakers Books, I volunteered to execute this audacious plan. My imprint publishes books about personal and social transformation, and I already knew many authors with exactly the kinds of expertise we needed. That's how the Resilience series was born.

I was overwhelmed by my authors' responses. Ten of them immediately said yes and agreed to the impossible deadline. The book you hold in your hands is the result of this intensive, collaborative effort. On behalf of John, myself, the authors and production team, our intention for you is that you take to heart the skills and techniques offered to you in this these pages. Master them. Make yourself stronger. Share your newfound resilience with those around you. Together, we can not only survive, but learn how to thrive in tough times. By so doing, we can find our way to a better future.

Tim Ward
Publisher, Changemakers Books

Introduction

"We've never been through anything like this before."

To hear it from my parents, both in their 80s, hit me hard. They've been through so much, but nothing like this.

I've started to wake up in the middle of the night and I crawl off alone, exhausted, after dinner. My wife is on the third floor on Zoom, holding meetings for hours on end and pleading for a cup of coffee. Our daughter, who is nine, misses her friends. I never thought we'd home school her, or that I'd be teaching math and social studies. But everybody home schools now. Last night she wanted to cuddle on the couch, all three of us, and watch a show we watched when she was three. She said nothing. She didn't sing the songs. This morning she crawled into bed and apologized. I asked what for. She said everything. She's been having headaches. She knows. We've never been through anything like this before.

At first it was inconvenient and a little boring. We wrote up schedules and ignored the fact that each day it felt like each room in the house was getting smaller. We took out the dogs and found fewer people out with each walk. The pub on the corner closed and the one on 2nd Street tried takeout for a few days but couldn't manage. No one is set up for this.

I know something is coming. I feel a rumbling of unsettled anxiety. I'm sluggish when I exercise, and I'm buzzing like I've had too much coffee when I'm not. My temper is getting short and my gut hurts after I eat. I definitely don't want a glass of wine, but I drink one anyway. I put down the book I've been reading and pick up a collection of horror stories. This is familiar. I know exactly what's happening. I *have* been through this before. The clues course through my body.

I write about anxiety, depression and bipolar disorder from a perspective of one who deals with these illnesses in his own life. Over the years I have put together a simple method of therapies that can help a person with these challenges manage life successfully. These therapies, centered on movement, meditation, and meaningful work, are just as powerful for people who do not have mental illness but still struggle to handle the daily challenges of anxiety in a time of crisis.

This is that time. None of us have ever been through anything like this before.

In all the darkness there is light. Incredible innovation sets up a hopeful future. New medical advances are announced each day, and factories are quickly re-tooled to make needed equipment. But still, no end to the pandemic is in sight. Every day the statistics bring unimaginable numbers, and every time the date the restrictions will be lifted is pushed back our anxiety deepens. Today the state where I live stopped delaying that date and just closed things indefinitely.

At once, anxiety is a collective and an individual experience. As a group we need to work together to defeat this common enemy. Individually we must face the causes of our anxiety and make life choices that will set us up for health and success. For ourselves and for our families.

There are ways one can see anxiety coming, and there are ways to intervene to head off a difficult episode that if uninterrupted can lead to physical illness, depression or other mood challenges. The secret is to get out of our heads and into our bodies. However, today's events conspire to keep us trapped within emotions that trouble our minds, and the physical illness seems to come only after we fall apart. In fact, dis-ease in our bodies often comes early and can tip us off to trouble in advance of the anxiety. If we know how to pay attention.

Handling Anxiety in a Time of Crisis is a guide to understanding and noticing the changes in the body that come before a difficult emotional episode. The book describes the progression of somatic changes that occur before full-blown anxiety kicks in and gives instructions on techniques you can use to notice these changes. Ideas on how to intervene once a mood swing seems imminent are offered as well.

Joining the discomfort we feel in our bodies as anxiety seizes us are thoughts we repeat over and over that make things seem worse than they often are. There are ways to notice this and settle your mind into a more assured, less uncertain ally. There is a course to wellness that we can navigate if we discover subtle changes in our body and thoughts. We can avoid severe anxiety if we know where to look and what to look for.

In a situation like the current pandemic, or in any period of crisis, anxiety is a given. We can keep it from disrupting our lives and making us less likely to meet the demands of each day. Times of great anxiety are here. It's a challenge for people with anxiety disorders, but even psychologically healthy people are finding their moods are getting the better of them. They, too, can benefit from this book.

My neighbor just knocked on the door so we could talk from across the street. Her routine's been up-ended and she feels like she's coming apart. My wife and I both broke down and cried this afternoon. My own moods, jostled by my bipolar disorder, are all over the place. Uncertainty is our common experience and anxiety is the emotion we all share. No, we have never been through anything like this before. But we can handle it.

Chapter One

What is Anxiety?

Anxiety in and of itself is not a bad thing. Someone has to worry about paying the bills, and someone has to have just enough fear to make sure the doors are locked and everyone is safe at night. There are reasons to be cautious and reasons to be careful. Anxiety, in fair amounts, helps us make good decisions and stay well.

If you're facing a situation that calls for caution or restraint, don't panic if a little anxiety makes you delay your response or seek more information before you commit. It's natural to look up the side effects of a new medicine your doctor wants you to take, and it's prudent to want to get to know your child's friends and their parents before the kids have a sleepover.

People have always been anxious, and there are good reasons the emotion has stayed with us. Our ancestors, living in tribes in the wilderness, faced all sorts of threats. A troubled person who would sit up all night and cry out at the sign of a predator was a valuable member of the group. A sensible touch of anxiety is one of the reasons why we're still here.

Too much anxiety, however, can strike us frozen with fear, crippled by concern, unable to get through a day without becoming mentally or physically sick. While you may think that your anxiety is some exaggerated character flaw that tortures you worse than anyone else, rest assured that many people experience anxiety that disrupts their lives. And understand that, even though anxiety can lock you into fearful inaction, it comes from a perfectly natural place: Your nervous system.

When our ancestors encountered a threat, their nervous systems kicked into overdrive. The perception of the threat caused adrenaline to shoot through them. Blood rushed to large muscles and vital organs. The airways in their lungs opened up. Their senses heightened and became sharper. Nutrients filled the bloodstream and their bodies became pumped up with energy. This complex reaction, which we still experience, happens in an instant. In fact, it happens so fast that the body is in full defensive mode even before the brain completely recognizes the threat. That's why you seemingly automatically steer away from a car that quickly enters your lane. You don't even think about it. This life-preserving function of our bodies is called the fight or flight response.

As quick as the body is to jump to a ready defensive reaction, it calms down when the danger passes. The high state of alert dissipates as the threat is removed. This all served us very well when we lived in nature and the threats were big and scary and could eat us. Because of the fight or flight response we could escape a predator or kill it and eat it. When the threat was neutralized we could relax and, sometimes, feast. Everything returned to normal.

Our physiology remains intact, and we share the fight or flight response with our ancestors. Only today the threats, the stress events, are much different. They may not be immediately life-threatening, but they don't just go away, either. Worry about trouble at work, or an ill child, or a bill you just can't pay doesn't dissipate. There is no resting and feasting because these threats don't quickly pass. They seem to drag on forever, and our bodies remain on high alert, constantly stressed. It makes us sick.

Uncertainty, boredom, the assault of assertive media and the constant contradictions of a terror filled world all trigger the fight or flight response. A quarantine in a collapsing economy threatened by an unfamiliar virus we're only aware of when symptoms appear causes these negations to persist. We have no idea when it all will end. We're on high alert in a desperate place where what inevitably happens seems completely out of our control. And to find yourself in a bad situation over which you have no control might be the most anxiety provoking threat of all. Despair makes us doubly anxious. The anxiety deepens the despair. The cycle swirls like a tornado that can pick up everything in its path, everything we thought was stable, and toss it around like matchsticks.

The catch is that while the fight or flight response and the anxiety it triggers is a physical experience, our minds often make it worse through worry, exaggeration, and stories with outright falsehoods that we tell ourselves. The difference between anxiety that we quickly dispel and anxiety that just grinds on without end is a matter of where the threat we perceive is located. When something external that we don't have time to think about causes the anxiety, like the car that swerves into our lane or the bear that threatens the camp, goes away, so does the anxiety. Things quickly return to normal. But when the anxiety becomes internalized, when negative thoughts clutch our minds, the fight or flight response takes hold and doesn't let go. Our thoughts perpetuate our suffering. Things don't get better until we go deep inside and deal with it.

The fight or flight response does not have to result in crippling anxiety. It is a part of being anxious, but it comes early and only sets the body up for the dis-ease of disruption. The mind has to take it from there. Stress that clouds our reason combines with our physiology to make life seem unbearable. As our mind convinces itself that things can't be fixed, the physiological response remains. Then life actually does become unbearable. The mind's certainty that all is wrong fuels the stress response in the body. The mind and the body, so well-tuned when they work together as one, seem to come apart and suddenly, through the constant replay of stressful thoughts, the mind is set against the body. Physical, and sometimes mental, illness follows.

The body easily falls ill as the assault of the mind drives a wedge between a person's perception of reality and what is actually happening around them. We get to the point where we don't trust our own thoughts. All the while the fight or flight response recycles without relief. The constant feeling on edge, the relentless rush of adrenaline, the disruption of sleep and normal functioning pulls the body and mind further apart.

The only way to overcome and correct this battle between the body and the mind is to rejoin the two. To make us comfortable in our body and confident in our thoughts. To reestablish the trust and harmony between the mental and the physical.

To eliminate a predator is easy. To get over fear, uncertainty and negativity takes a set of skills many of us don't naturally possess. We have an incredible talent we can use to handle anxiety. We can learn.

Episodes of Anxiety

Anxiety has become a catch-all word for the on-edge, out of control feelings we encounter in the face of some daunting challenge. These feelings change from a normal, beneficial response to a pathological problem when the emotions and the moods they cause become irrational; unsuited to the stressors that present themselves.

We've all been there. Anxiety is a common experience. Yet it is an interior expression of heightened fear. We each know what it is, but when we're in the worst of it it's isolating. We encounter these fears and dysfunctions completely alone. That feeling of being completely by ourselves, battered by panicky thoughts and unnerving discomfort, only makes things worse. Almost all of us share this experience, especially in times of crisis. We hold up the cool hero, unfazed by constant trouble, as the example of how we should face crisis. But in fact, we've each been to the point at which we've stumbled. The hero we idolize is an archetype of mythology.

For most people coming apart is an infrequent event. It happens, and it's important to learn how to deal with it, but it seldom upends our lives. When it does happen, as in the unsettling disruptions to our lives during the Covid-19 pandemic, it often happens to many of us at once. But even in these cases, anxiety remains a private suffering few of us are prepared to deal with. It's lonely, and it hurts.

For a significant number of people, though, anxiety becomes disabling. Whether diagnosed as social anxiety, obsessive compulsive disorder, panic disorder, or specific phobias, anxiety can be an illness that requires medical treatment. Anxiety left unchecked can develop into generalized anxiety disorder, the feeling of high anxiety on most days for a period of six months or more. Fear and worry rule our days and influence every decision we make, if we're able to make decisions at all. In cases like this, professional help from a doctor or therapist is warranted.

When feelings of uncertainty pervade every experience we have and every decision we're called on to consider, anxiety quickly becomes dysfunctional. In times of crisis like the one we face today, whether we're unsure of our next paycheck or worrying if we, our children or our parents will fall ill, or even in doubt as to when we'll be able to get out and see friends again, anxiety can quickly cripple us. It's especially cruel because once anxiety has us, when we're able to make quick decisions or significant plans, we often make bad ones. Fear and worry inhibit our best potential and keep us trapped inside.

But we can deal with it. Anxiety is often episodic. It pops up at unfortunate times, ruins things for a while, and then goes away. Left injured, we anticipate it coming back. This anticipation may actually invite anxiety right back in as the high state of alert, this fear of repeat, stresses us again to the point of illness. It's a cycle we have to learn to manage. We can intervene before or between episodes. We have to develop an awareness of our state between episodes and prepare to act when we feel anxiety coming on again.

Anxiety Can Aggravate Other Conditions

Anxiety is one of the affective disorders. It often occurs with and can seriously aggravate the other two: depression and bipolar disorder. More than 50% of people diagnosed with either depression or bipolar disorder also have an anxiety disorder. Even in those without a diagnosed anxiety disorder, feelings of anxiety can bring about or exacerbate an episode of depression or mania.

In my personal experience with bipolar disorder, my worst episodes often begin with an overwhelming sense of anxiety. An unsettled, jumpy feeling keeps me on edge. My sleep is disrupted, if I can sleep at all. I feel a sense of foreboding, and trepidation keeps me from doing things that, without the anxiety, I really enjoy doing. The episodes are so similar early on that it's often difficult to tell the difference between an anxiety attack and a mixed-state of depression and mania.

Anxiety also fuels panic attacks. During a very difficult time with my bipolar disorder, just days after being released from the hospital, I sat in church for Mass. The priest made a joke about bipolar disorder. Suddenly everything in that safe quiet place became a threat. The organ seemed to drone out of tune and the light shot like strobes through the stained-glass windows. People in the congregation seemed to double over with laughter. In full panic, all I could do was get out. I ran into the parking lot and collapsed in fear. The panic passed and the anxiety eased. I realized I needed more help in order to cope.

Fortunately, the methods I describe in this book work to offset all types of difficult episodes. I use them now on a regular basis and I feel a lot safer.

Several physical health diseases also commonly join with anxiety. Anxiety contributes to heart and lung disease, gastrointestinal distress and chronic pain. It makes symptoms worse for the patient and can delay a recovery from the physical disorder. An anxiety attack will quicken the pulse and lead to shortness of breath. When my daughter was two, I felt a strange tingling and shooting pain in my left arm and shoulder. I began to sweat and get dizzy. My chest ached. A neighbor rushed over to stay with my daughter until my wife could race home from work, and I took a cab to the hospital. Yes, it would have made more sense to call 911, but the hospital is only twelve blocks away and I wasn't thinking right. In the ER they rushed me to the cardiac unit and started tests and treatment. It was an anxiety attack.

Stress and anxiety have also plagued my mid-section. Pains that can make me keel over sometime assault my bowels. This is not uncommon. When nervous or panicked, the body often expresses itself in the gastro-intestinal tract. In fact, the enteric nervous system intimately connects the brain with the gut and strongly impacts emotions and moods. Anxiety that starts in your brain is often first felt in your gut. Whether you call it butterflies or irritable bowel syndrome or agita, our intestines suffer the stress. Feelings of discomfort in the gut can also influence the expression of anxiety in your mind. We can feel the fear and worry in our gut. You need to pay special attention to your abdomen in ferreting out and treating anxiety.

Anxiety is not all in your head. It will not make you crazy. By itself it will not kill you. But it can complicate other conditions that can make you very sick. Anxiety is a physical disorder with physical symptoms. While it is aggravated by thoughts and perceptions, it needs to be treated as a physical illness as well as a mental illness. For at its very core, anxiety is a physical experience.

Approaching anxiety as a physical experience should not emphasize the separation of mind and body that has distracted and damaged us for centuries. It should help us reconcile the two. Anxiety crushes the heart and confuses the mind. Interestingly, in biblical Hebrew the word leb meant both heart and mind. No distinction was made between the two. To properly handle anxiety today we need to reunite them, to view the heart and mind again as one. There is no clearer example than anxiety of how, when one is sick, so, equally, is the other.

Anxiety may be indicative of a battle waged between the heart and the mind. It is what happens when one does not pay attention to the other. If we want to correct our mind, we have to listen to our body. The mind, especially when anxious, tends to jump all over the place and can be incredibly inconsistent. Feelings in the body are easier to identify and may tell us more about the state of our health. In learning to handle anxiety, we should begin there.

I write of handling anxiety as opposed to overcoming it because the first step is to dispel the notion that you're at war with yourself. You're not to fight your way through this. You have to hold yourself gently and understand that you're just suffering from a normal function that has gone a little haywire. Arguing with yourself about the accuracy of your thoughts is unlikely to yield positive results. It's not always possible to take a step back and consider where you may be wrong. In the grip of anxiety you're probably too self-critical and too negative to be objective about yourself, anyway.

In order to best live in anxious times we'll have to read our body as we approach each threat. The predator at the door is extremely real, and extreme reactions to deal with it are expected. But uncertainty, worry about things that might or might not happen, and fear of the unknown do not call for immediate, highly stressed action. We should pause. Experience the sensations in our bodies. Carefully consider things. Plan a little. Anxiety, unfortunately, often makes this impossible.

When our thought patterns are broken we can still find the way to health. We must search deep within our bodies to discover how we truly feel and what we must do about it. Anxiety is physical. Thoughts just make it worse. We must first work with the body to come to terms with it. We'll get to the thoughts later.

For in the words of Richard Rohr, "You cannot think yourself into new ways of living, but you can live yourself into new ways of thinking."

Key Takeaways

- Anxiety is a natural, protective emotion
- The fight or flight response fuels anxiety
- Uncertainty can lead to dysfunctional anxiety
- Anxiety can aggravate other health conditions

Chapter Two

How to Recognize Anxiety

Anxiety hits hard, and its symptoms are unmistakable. Even so, sometimes in the rush and confusion of uncertainty we miss them, or don't attribute them to challenging mental health, until it's too late. Still, there are ways to recognize that anxiety is coming before it seizes you. Look out for some of the more common physical symptoms. The list is long, and symptoms vary for each individual. But we'll learn how to notice which symptoms affect you. The list includes:

* * *

Chronic or sudden pain; loss of color in the face; trembling or tingling in the hands or feet; tightness in the chest; clumsiness; dizziness; feeling faint; headaches; heart palpitations or pounding; excess energy; fatigue; muscle tension; nausea; nervous cough; night sweats; restless leg syndrome; sexual dysfunction; weight changes.

* * *

Once you identify your symptoms, you can notice them early and then you can intervene with some key techniques to avoid the worst of a brewing episode. You can make anxiety less severe when it appears, or even avoid it altogether.

Remember that anxiety is a physiological response. It is most certainly not all in your head. Don't blame yourself when you feel it coming. You haven't done anything wrong, and you're not weak. Even when you crumble under the weight of extreme anxiety.

The key to identifying physical symptoms and accurately predicting oncoming episodes of anxiety is body awareness.

While thoughts can aggravate feelings of anxiety, and we must deal with these thoughts, we must first consider the physical aspects of anxiety. And the physical warning signs that it is coming. To do this you must pay attention to your body. You must contemplate your entire experience, not just what is going on from your shoulders up. You must get out of your head and pay attention to the rest of you.

If you exercise, focus on how your body feels. Practice movement with a purpose for a while. Forget about your VO2 max or racing to the top of your spin class. Turn off the music and the computer or TV. Just move, by yourself, in silence. Identify where in your body you feel tension and where you feel relaxed. Investigate the quality of your breath. Is it deep and full? Is it short and clipped? Are you comfortable or are you gasping? Just consider how being alone with yourself moving, without all the overstimulation, feels.

We spend so little time in our bodies that when we open up to our physical experience it can be enlightening. This practice may be both liberating and natural. Or you may find this time spent moving without a goal anxiety provoking itself. If that's the case, take a break and consider why.

I like to learn stuff, so when I'm exercising I often put on some online course and amble through the motions. The movement just becomes automatic and the voice of the teacher a distraction. Most of the time I'm not really paying attention to either. My mind wanders and I move without purpose. Before I know it, it's done. In the end I haven't learned much of anything about my body or the subject matter of the course.

This is when it's time to go for a walk without the phone. Without the earbuds. Just me. You should try the same.

Pay attention to how you feel: Your feet on the sidewalk; your arms swinging at your shoulders; your knees flexing, and any breeze you feel on your face. Be deliberate. Take each step carefully and bring your full attention to each footfall. Sure, you'll get lost in thought, but pay attention to what you're feeling as well as you can. When your mind does wander, bring it back to the feelings in your legs or upper-body or the increasing rhythm of your breath. And when you find yourself off again, completely lost in your thoughts, because your mind would rather do anything than pay attention to something as automatic and familiar as walking, stop for a moment and stand still. Place your mind in the soles of your feet. Push off with one foot (trust me, if you really think about this when you do it, it will feel awkward) and begin walking again. Feel the muscles in your calves and thighs working. Feel your breath and your pulse begin to pick up. Yes, you'll get lost in your thoughts again, but when you notice that you have, stop again and start over. Don't worry that to anyone watching you may look silly. You do. Enjoy it.

If it seems like I'm turning walking into a meditation, that's because I am. Here's the reason. If anxiety does come on you need to notice it in your body first in order to do anything in time to prevent it. To do this you must be comfortable in your body and fully aware of how you feel. Your mind wants to hog all the attention and your body often moves unnoticed. You have to change that. You may even find it feels pretty good.

Once you develop the ability to pay attention to how your body feels while just walking, standing and walking again, you can take this body focus into other forms of movement. Or, like me, you can just keep on walking. I add a short routine of stretching and calisthenics to my daily practice and I'm set. It keeps me fit, and it keeps me focused on how my body feels.

Learning to meditate while moving is safer than classic seated meditation if you're prone to anxiety and have trouble managing extreme stress. Sitting still and ruminating about all your problems and how bad and scary everything is isn't going to help you at all at this point. We'll get to that later.

When you're comfortable in your body, and I mean comfortable about how you measure your feelings, not how you look, you'll begin to notice things. You'll notice when you're calm or edgy, tired or wide awake. You'll begin to get a pretty good handle on your mood just by paying attention to your body. Take special note of where you ache and how you feel in your heart and in your gut. This is where anxiety is going to show up first.

When you've become adept at walking, without too many distractions, while paying attention to your full self, you may find that the terrible thoughts that have been chasing you, the ones that really make you anxious, begin to slow down. You may even get out ahead of them and lose them for a while. Oh, they'll come back, but at least you'll develop a sense that now you can have some control over them.

Try it for a few days. Walking alone outside without distractions, except for your own thoughts, might be the only meditation practice you need. You may feel better. This may be enough to help you truly understand how you feel. Your sense of anxiety may settle, at least for a while. Walking each day can do this. You may even want to get a dog.

If you're a runner you can bring this same practice to your running. If you usually run with earbuds and music, go out without them. It still helps to fully come into your body by walking first. Work up to your own pace and take it from there.

If this practice is helping, if it feels good at all (or maybe even if it doesn't), it's time to try something else. Standing still.

This is a more formal meditation, but one that still enables you to come deeply into your body and truly experience all that you feel. And some of what you think. Try it out.

Stand barefoot with your feet shoulder width apart and let your hands fall naturally to your sides. Pull your shoulders back slightly and don't lock your knees. Keep them soft throughout. Posture is important, but you don't have to be military formal. Close the eyes if you can, or simply hold the gaze in soft focus at a spot on the floor a few feet in front of you. Keep your head up.

Pull up and gently drop the shoulders two or three times, and take a few deep breaths. Check the knees to see if they have locked, and relax the shoulders.

Stand in silence for a few minutes, first feeling the muscles in the feet constantly adjust, different parts of the sole in contact with the floor at different times as the body keeps its balance. Feel into the calves as the body settles in. Check the knees and shoulders again. The knees may keep locking and the shoulders may keep creeping up toward the ears. Relax. Stand in silence for a few minutes. Really try this. Don't read on until you have. You'll spoil the fun.

I bet you were surprised at how much you move by just standing still. The body moves around a lot, as if the legs are the trunk of a tree and the upper body the branches swaying in the wind. As the body constantly adjusts and rebalances some people even experience a bit of motion sickness. It's always a surprise to feel this. I've practiced this way countless times and it still impresses me. Apparently, there is no such thing as truly standing still.

Loosen your knees again and reposition your shoulders. Stand quietly for a few more minutes.

Take a deep breath. Roll your shoulders backwards a few times, and then forward. Stretch your neck slowly, carefully, from side to side, then front to back. Check your knees and shoulders again. Feel your feet, calves and thighs. Take another deep breath, and go ahead and slowly sit down.

People are often astounded to discover how much goes into just standing still. They're struck by all the things they never noticed, especially all the swaying, while doing something they've done all their lives. This shows you the incredible power of discovery, and the ability to notice new things when you focus your attention on your body.

If by standing still for a few minutes you can notice things your body does that you've missed your entire life, imagine how you can develop the ability to notice slight or profound changes in your body that may signal an episode of anxiety is imminent.

Just pay attention, and as you practice daily note when things feel different. When things feel odd, do any unusual thoughts bubble up? When you focus on an area of tension or discomfort does your mind change? This can be very telling.

At a more basic level note the things you feel that signal that you're stressed. I find I'll get a knot in my left shoulder and a cramping and popping in my left jaw. My forehead and my brow feel tight. Most alarming is discomfort in the right side of my abdomen. It can actually harden, ball up and sharply hurt.

In just going through the motions from day to day I often notice none of this until it's too late. Before I know it anxiety or some other mood change strikes. But if I practice in my body through movement or standing still, I know when a challenging time is coming. I feel it early. I know what to do. You can develop this skill too.

Turning Your Attention from Your Body to Your Mind

Once you're fully aware of your body and how it feels, you can begin to recognize when anxiety begins to creep from your body into your mind. Tuned into how you feel, you'll notice when you're ill at ease in your body first.

Then it's time to determine what threat your brain has perceived to cause this dis-ease in your body. As much as it is comfortable, turn your attention from your body to your mind. Notice the thoughts you're having, especially the ones that repeat and trouble you. If your thoughts become uncomfortable, turn your attention back to your body and survey how you feel. Have you tightened up? Do you feel sick? Are you on edge?

If while walking or standing you feel tension or discomfort in a specific part of your body, pause for a moment. Stay still. Imagine directing the breath into that part of the body and fill the tense area with the inhale. Hold it for a moment. Relax the tense area into the exhale. Repeat this a few times and you may feel the tension release. Learn where in the body you hold your stress, and pay attention to that spot(s) when you practice.

Try it for a few minutes and see. Stand again (you can do this practice seated or even lying down but for now just stand). Relax and place your attention on your breath. Feel the inhale enter the body, pause for a moment, and release without effort into the exhale. Breathe this way for a minute or two. Think of an area in your body that often aches or feels tense when you're highly stressed.

Turn the attention to this part of your body. Consider how it feels right now. You may find a bit of discomfort or serious tension. Or you may feel fine. Either way, hold this area of your body in focus. As you inhale, direct the full breath toward this part of your body. Breathe right into the area that pains you. Hold it for a moment. Experience fully how you feel.

Now, with a sense of full relaxation, allow the exhale to flow slowly and completely out of this spot and out of the body. Pause again and repeat. Here, instead of breathing naturally, make each breath purposefully deep. Complete the cycle five or six times. Return to a natural breath, and let the focus on the body go. Note how you feel, and what you may be thinking. Notice if other areas of stress have popped up in your body. If they have, attend to them with the same practice. When through just relax and get on with your day. If you've had any profound thoughts write them down and save them for later. Just relax for now.

Often, just by noticing feelings of discomfort and attending to them with the breath you can settle down. The power of your attention and your ability to place it where you wish is undeniable. At times, just focusing the attention on something that feels bad and spending some time with it until you fully experience these feelings will help you relax and feel better. Like me, with these practices you can begin to listen to and comprehend your body.

Your thoughts are a little more difficult.

Unlike the practice in the body, sometimes focusing your attention on your thoughts will just make you feel awful. Just remember, if you don't like what's going on in your head, you can always turn your attention back to your body and re-set. Take a deep breath. Rotate your shoulders. Touch your toes. Take a few more deep breaths. Begin to pay attention to your thoughts through walking and standing meditation. Don't sit still just yet, unless you have an established practice. Occupying part of the brain with the task of keeping you balanced will make it easier to focus on and deal with your thoughts. And if you're distressed and need to back away from a train of thoughts, the body will be more available for you to retreat into if it's engaged in activity.

An ability to bring your attention back to your body will also help you overcome feelings that you are inadequate to meet the task of coping with uncertainty. Early in anxiety, when the wash of emotion is pulling back along the shore to gather force and rise up and crash on you like a wave, it is natural to feel like you're not up to the task. What comes next is the feeling that you just can't take it. But if you can exist in your body instead of in your head at just this time you'll catch yourself if you slip into volumes of negative self-talk.

This negative talk may be ramblings about how terrible you feel physically and/or mentally. You may be locked on the uncertainty of the moment of crisis and doubting your ability to handle the situation. Worry for family members and friends, or for all people affected by the crisis, may seize your mind and infuse every waking moment. Come back to your body.

If you can focus on the physical you'll be able to disengage from these thoughts and settle into your body, which is fine just the way it is. Feelings of inadequacy will pass and a resolve to go on will be born. Then you can regroup, pull away from your body, and safely return to your thoughts.

When you think about your thinking, you're looking for clues as to what is driving your anxiety. When you're able to calmly assess thoughts that repeat and thoughts that make you upset, you might be surprised at what lurks behind them. It's often an exaggeration or one big lie you're telling yourself. We'll encounter such false thoughts in the next chapter.

We've all had the experience of feeling so anxious that we thought we were going to die. But we didn't die. Our thoughts had us convinced that it was all over and we just couldn't take anymore. Our bodies ached and we may even have gotten physically ill. Panic attacks may have beset us. But we didn't die. Our thoughts, as inaccurate and ill-reasoned as they were, convinced us that it was lights out. Either something shocked us back into reality or we just burned out from the spent adrenaline, but we recovered. In all likelihood our life after the anxiety attack was just like our life before it.

Thoughts, for a moment, can change everything. Everything in us can seem to fall apart, even if everything external remains exactly the same. Mere thoughts can make us sick. But we don't just think ourselves into anxiety. Things happen in our bodies: sensations we can identify and work with. Then something within us can rise up and counter those disruptive thoughts. Suddenly things will just seem better. We can overcome the fight or flight response and observe the anxiety dissipate.

Our moods don't have to be so surprising and so beyond our control. When anxiety strikes there are actions we can take so that ill health, or recovery, doesn't just happen by chance.

Key Takeaways

- Physical symptoms signal anxiety
- Recognizing these symptoms early can help avoid extreme anxiety
- Walking and standing meditation can help predict the onset of anxiety
- This can allow the meditator to uncover the mental causes of anxiety

Chapter Three

What to Do When Anxiety Comes

Depression is the past. Anxiety is the future.

When anxiety moves from the body into the mind it often begins with a sense of foreboding about what's to come. We feel like we've lost control of even the most basic things in our lives, and the future becomes more of a threat than a promise. The worst feeling in the world may be to have no idea what is going to happen to you and your family, and to not know what to do about any of the possible outcomes. But this is what anxiety serves us.

In a crisis, questions are all we have. If our leaders are unsure of themselves or inconsistent in their proclamations and actions it only adds to the uncertainty we already feel. If the crisis directly affects us or people we are close to it roosts too close to home to allow us to be sure of anything.

Strangers can become a threat, and we retreat into a posture of defense, always on guard, unreasonably tense. We lose all flexibility. So rigid and full of questions, we can only break. Unless we take some early actions and, while continuing to care for those close to us, institute some practices to take care of ourselves as well.

There are some simple things we should do that in stable times would seem obvious, but in the fist of anxiety all is so easily forgotten. In a state of high anxiety, even simple things can feel far too difficult to implement. But you can and you must try. If you can't find it within yourself to take these steps quickly, think of the others who need you and do it for them. Don't get lost too deep within yourself.

These are obvious, normal things to do that in anxiety may seem daunting. In anxiety, nothing is normal, and little seems obvious but the things you are afraid of – most of which aren't even real. But we'll get to that.

To begin, here are some of the things you should do to stave off anxiety or keep a moderate case of anxiety, which is normal and even expected in a time of crisis, from becoming seriously disabling.

First, guard your sleep. Keep as regular a schedule as you can. Go to bed at the same time each evening (and don't stay up too late) and get up at the same time each morning. Shower, groom and dress each day. You must establish a routine, especially if the routine you are used to has been disrupted. Design and adhere to a new one. The best first step toward establishing a new routine is to schedule your sleep. If sleep becomes difficult, don't load yourself up with additional things to do at the time you should be in bed. Rest. You'll need it.

Avoid substances. I have a neighbor who says drinking helps with his anxiety. The key he says is to drink like Goldilocks. Not too little, not too much. This is a terrible idea. If you're used to having a glass of wine with dinner or a beer after work, that's fine. To stop now would be to violate an enjoyable part of your routine. But don't start drinking more. Alcohol is a central nervous system depressant. It may feel good while you're drinking, but it has a cumulative effect that will get you. And then you'll just feel worse.

A friend I know says smoking pot relaxes him. In a state of anxiety, however, remember that cannabis is a psychoactive drug. If paranoia is part of your anxiety, pot will only make it worse. It can also aggravate other emotional or psychiatric difficulties you may be having.

Someone else I know puts CBD drops on his ice cream. CBD is largely untested and unregulated, and we really have no idea whether it helps or hurts general health. Any substance you introduce to your body can affect your emotions. Best to leave it alone.

Only take prescription sleep aids if your doctor has prescribed them for you. Only take other medicines exactly as prescribed. You're strong enough to face this crisis without adding non-prescribed or mind-altering drink and drugs. You need your wits about you to stay at your best, or to return to your best. In a crisis there are surely people who depend on you. Stay sober for them. You don't want to make yourself feel numb. It honestly won't help.

To continue to feel vital you should exercise and eat well. Remember, movement can help your body and your mind. It is a crucial part of measuring your mood and remaining healthy. Even if you're stuck inside and can't get to your gym, exercise. If you need a class or a trainer you can find one online. If you can go it alone as I've described, great. You can stay alert, fit and reap all the rewards detailed in the previous chapter.

Avoid junk food. It will make you feel emotionally and physically lethargic. If acquiring food is difficult, or if your favorite restaurants are closed, keep it basic and work with what you've got. Just avoid the fatty, sugary, salty stuff. Get some fresh fruits and vegetables. Consider probiotics to help with the mind-gut connection, and don't forget the protein. Take this extra time at home to cook healthy homemade meals. Follow online tutorials and experiment, even if you have little experience cooking.

Do something creative and try to stay busy. A key part of your routine should not be time spent just sitting around doing nothing (meditation counts as doing something). Read or play games to stimulate your mind. Binge watch a show? Sure, but be sure to limit it. You need activity so don't spend too much time on the couch with the remote. Entertainment is fine, but not all the time. Be creative yourself. Listen to music or play an instrument. Paint or build something. Dance around the living room. Make sure you keep working and remain productive. If you're working from home you may have to schedule some down time. If you're home schooling and working you may feel overwhelmed. Make sure everyone is chipping in with the chores, and teach your kids some life skills. Cook together, fold laundry together, clean out the closet together. Work will help you in ways beyond the obvious financial ones. Work is necessary for wellbeing. If you're without work take up a hobby. Create something. Stay engaged. Share your work with those around you. Use this time to grow.

There are so many opportunities for growth. If you can get a break and have some down time countless activities are available online. If you're out of work and unsure of your future in your career, you especially need the distraction and enrichment of ongoing development. Fill up your days. Much of what you'll find online is free. Tutorials for every hobby you ever wanted to explore are on YouTube, and groups that share information and camaraderie are formed daily.

In pursuing new challenges don't forget your body. Home gyms are delivered every day, but you don't need equipment and you don't need to spend. Just move. Again, so much inspiration and instruction for every possible exercise is available online. Exercise can provide a great opportunity to get outside and breathe fresh air. As I write it's spring, and every walk every day brings new buds on the trees and new flowers breaking through the soil.

Work, especially creative work, paid or hobby, can be a key exercise in focused attention. You can make productive work, especially physical work like cooking and housework, a sort of meditation. And like meditation, work will help you with the emotional effects of anxiety and restore and maintain your mental and physical health. Plus, you'll have a nicer space to live in and better tasting meals to eat.

Thoughts and Anxiety

The symptoms of anxiety that trouble your mind and your

emotions can be the most serious. The establishment of a routine and the maintenance of a productive lifestyle will go a long way toward avoiding or properly dealing with these, as will the walking, standing and classic seated meditation described throughout this book. But still, these symptoms will likely challenge you at some point during a period of anxiety in a time of crisis, or anxiety at any time.

Common though difficult psychological experiences with anxiety include:

* * *

Difficulty thinking; easy distraction; a fear of going crazy or losing control; fear of impending doom; memory loss; racing thoughts; ruminating; crying for no reason; mood swings; feeling numb; believing everything is a threat; irritability; an overwhelming urge to run away.

* * *

When you come up against these symptoms continue to hold to the recommendations cited above. Continue to practice movement and manage the physical symptoms of anxiety. And begin to gently, carefully, but with confidence, confront the emotions that trouble your mind, and the veracity of the self-talk that undergirds the emotions.

Be cautious of being too cautious. The voice in your head may coerce you into a corner of fear and prevent you from facing the challenges that confront you. Don't talk yourself out of good ideas or workable solutions. Consider reason over inaction. Try to notice if negativity is causing you more anxiety.

Investigate your negative thoughts. You're probably fearing the worst, and the worst will probably never happen. Determine which negative thoughts are generated within you and which are external and placed into your mind by others or the media. Don't constantly watch the news. It's important to be informed during a crisis. It's important to know what's going on and what the probable outcomes are. This is crucial to keeping your perspective.

By nature our minds will jump to the worst case scenario and exaggerate all threats. The worst rarely happens. Realize the range of possibilities the current crisis presents you and prepare for the most likely. Trustworthy sources of news and statistics can offer you parameters within which you can plan. You don't have to hear it over and over again, day after day. Take in just enough news to satisfy your curiosity and help you keep reasonable expectations. Be careful of your sources. Don't believe unsupported claims or conjecture. Rely on trusted sources like the CDC, the WHO or local authorities. Sources that change their tune constantly or contradict the experts are not to be trusted.

Our world of social media and 24-hour cable news has created an environment in which everyone has something to say and the means to say it. Often the news only reports, and people almost always repost the most sensational and most negative stories. So much that is posted is recycled BS that will only inflame your anxiety. On matters of science and policy we are not equal to the experts. Unfortunately, this world of constant rumor and misinformation, even lies floated as fact, has led us to mistrust everyone. Even experts. This does not help us temper anxiety in a crisis. It makes it worse. Remember, in a crisis some people do know better and ought to be listened to. Heed their recommendations. They will make you feel secure and, possibly, more certain. They have credentials. They don't speak in sensationalist platitudes. They're not shrill and rarely contradict themselves. And when they do, they rationally explain the reasons why. It's usually new information and always helpful. They're measured and while they do debate other experts, they don't make enemies. Choose wisely who to believe[1]. Distorted facts and disappointed expectations spread online or on TV will only prod your anxiety. Seek to know, but seek the truth. And keep it to just enough to satisfy you and make you feel informed and settled. You don't need more than that. Seek reassurance, but not every minute of the day.

Take Inventory of What You Have

It's common in a crisis to fear losing what's yours. It starts with your possessions, then your job and your health. It extends to those you love and, if you let it get the better of you, you fear losing your safety, your sanity or worse. Fear can get the better of you. Right now, where I live during the Covid-19 crisis, shops in Center City are boarding up their windows and doors. People are starting to assume the worst, and even though this is a public health crisis, distribution of goods is threatened and shopkeepers fear looting. The unemployment office is closed and the website for new claims keeps crashing. People are locked in place, with absolutely nowhere to turn.

In times like these it makes sense to take an honest inventory of what you have, both emotional and material, and what is most important to you. In doing so you'll likely realize that things are a lot more secure than you think. Some things, especially the love in your life, you will always have, no matter what happens. Many things will be different as the crisis passes. But people and things you care about will still be there. In the throes of anxiety it is difficult to see beyond all the change and loss, and the loss of routine, of what we thought was permanent. For all that we grieve.

The experience of grief drags us into the pit of the future and sets us down in an unfamiliar place where we lament the passing of the predictable. Even the most spontaneous among us craves, and clings to, some routine. Crisis can upend all of that.

The shock and denial of grief in anxiety hits all of us. Early in the pandemic we saw the virus as some distant pathogen wreaking havoc in some faraway land and we convinced ourselves it wouldn't come here. When it did many of us spent a week or two going about our normal lives. Then it spiked, and we panicked. We emptied the shelves in overrun stores. We retreated into safe spaces and still felt uncomfortable. Even at home.

Fueling anxiety today is a tremendous sense of guilt. Our kids are home but we're working, too, and not spending enough time with them. We're not making time for the expansive loving connections they keep talking about on TV. We're just getting by, if we're getting by at all. Others aren't getting by, even a little. Those less fortunate, those more vulnerable and more exposed, have fewer resources and fewer options. We must keep them in mind and always remember that to suffer is universal. The people close to me have each other and most of us are safe. But anxiety whispers to us it's not enough. We must do more. We're failing those we love. We're only safe for now.

I don't see much anger around, except for that directed at politicians, who acted late and allowed this crisis to get away from them only to cede leadership and blame others. Amongst each other there is more cooperation and community than anger, although there is that touch of fear of the stranger who may infect us. On a personal scale we grieve in loneliness. Every passing day we make up new ways to stay connected to each other. In the past I turned bashing social media into a sport, but now I realize I was at least partially wrong. We've had game nights and play dates on Zoom. Church isn't so bad when you open the laptop, pour a cup of coffee and sit on your couch in your pajamas. Thank God this didn't happen just a few years ago when we had none of this technology. We'd be all alone, leaving home to walk the street desperate to see someone, spreading germs.

Many who grieve go to support groups. Today the world, if you scratch the surface and get online, is one big support group.

Everyone has been touched by coronavirus in very profound ways. People have cathartic stories to tell, some filled with pathos and some with joy, and they are hungry to tell them to you. All you have to do is ask. The connection you can make can approach the spiritual and, for a moment, in this incredible gift of connection, your grief will lift and the anxiety it makes simmer will flicker out. That's why, along with taking inventory of all you have, you must place your connection to others, and your ability to reach out to them, at the top of the list. We have each other. If you feel alone, search online for a shared community with similar interests and/or values. If you can't get online reach out to a neighbor. You can connect, even from six feet away. While we each may face this crisis differently, we're facing the same enemy. Survival free of anxiety is our common cause.

With all of this comes an inner dialogue that challenges us and every action we take. Can you meet the world as you? Doubt bedevils us. Uncertainty freezes us into inaction. We can have the physical, the material, the financial and the familial all in place, but our thoughts may not trust any of it. Despite all evidence to the contrary, anxiety can darken our world a hopeless black. Even when consciously aware that things are not as bad as they seem, our thoughts may still convince us otherwise. The kindling of anxiety is erroneous thought. Such thoughts take the discomfort in the body we've worked to heal and understand and turn it into panic. Thoughts will make us ill in ways that will leave us wretching in pain, emotional and physical. We can reconcile the objective and the subjective, but we should not do it from a place of dysfunction. We may need to call a therapist or a doctor on telehealth. For now, we can go back into our body and introduce the truth of lived experience to our mind. To accomplish this, they must meet in a neutral, controlled practice.

We can temper the negative thoughts and expose the lies and exaggerations we tell ourselves on an endless loop that repeats inside our heads. We can determine what in our self-judgment is true and what is false. We just need to keep paying attention, as we've learned so far, and add a little doubt. We have to fully experience our lives to find our truth and positively embrace and diminish our anxiety. The things we've practiced so far may be enough. Or we may have to sit down and breathe.

Key Takeaways

- Establish new routines in a disruptive crisis
- Stay focused, active and creative
- Take inventory of the things the crisis cannot take away
- If severe anxiety becomes disabling reach out to professional help

Chapter Four

Meditation and Anxiety

I've presented how you can turn movement and body awareness into a contemplative practice through which you can anticipate, and even gently dismiss, anxiety. But what about plain old meditation?

If you have a regular meditation practice then great, do it. You'll find yourself able to go deep into your body, often just by focusing on your breath, and feel anxiety as it begins to seep into your gut, shoulders, jaw and limbs. You'll also become adept at identifying thoughts and noticing how much unfounded fear and worry goes on in your head. Meditation can yield profound insight into how such inaccurate thoughts contribute to anxiety.

If you haven't meditated before you may benefit from trying it. Meditation holds many benefits for those struggling to handle anxiety. The obvious are stress management and improved focused. Others, such as the ability to predict difficult episodes, are also available to the meditator.

Meditation is quite different from sitting there doing nothing, thinking nothing. It is instead a focused attention on one's present experience. It offers you a chance to observe your thoughts and the feelings in your body, and to contemplate that thoughts that are so influential to your behavior may be full of lies about yourself and your situation.

It gives you the space to know and to change.

Meditation trains you to notice things you may have missed, and to find a still point in the onslaught of emotions painful or scattered anxiety may bring. Simple in practice, it still requires effort to achieve real benefits.

We know anxiety disorder is much more than being very nervous or edgy. In anxiety, a person will report an unreasonable exaggeration of threats, repetitive negative thinking, hyperarousal, and a strong identification with fear. The fight or flight response is kicked into overdrive and physical symptoms such as rapid heartbeat, high blood pressure, and digestive problems often precede the cognitive challenges that anxiety disorder presents. In anxiety the symptoms may become so severe that normal daily functioning becomes impossible.

Instead of changing the thoughts that herald anxiety, meditation seeks to change the relationship between the meditator and their thoughts. In meditation the person notices and focuses on physical feelings in the body that arise when they become anxious. Instead of avoiding or withdrawing from these feelings, the meditator remains present and fully experiences the symptoms of anxiety.

Instead of avoiding distressing thoughts, the meditator opens up to them in an effort to realize and acknowledge that they are not literally true. Although it may seem counterintuitive, fully realizing the experience of anxiety enables the meditator to release over identification with negative thoughts. The person practices responding to disruptive thoughts, and lets these thoughts go. By remaining present in the body, the meditator learns that the anxiety they experience is merely a reaction to perceived threats, and that by positively responding to threatening events instead of being reactive they can overcome an overactive fight or flight response fueled by false thoughts.

In beginning to diminish anxiety through meditation, it's important to know exactly how the anxiety feels, what physical symptoms lead up to it, and what thoughts that run through your mind make it worse. In other words, a way to reduce the symptoms of anxiety is to be fully, mindfully, anxious. As the cause of anxiety reveals itself to be misperception, symptoms will dissipate.

We've already learned how to identify and categorize the physical symptoms that arise in your body as you become anxious. You can continue to work with your body through movement or standing practice, or you can attempt to scan the body and look for areas of tension and other troubling sensations while seated. This body scan includes a survey of the areas in your body where you seem to hold tension and stress. A focus on these areas may bring underlying anxiety to the surface and enable you to relax and begin to explore thoughts that attach to your physical sensations.

Then, as you've noticed that anxiety is beginning to well up in you, you can review your thoughts for their accuracy. Anxiety may be a reasonable response to what's going on in the world affected by Covid-19 and the illness and distress, economic and social, that come with it. Some measure of anxiety is to be expected. But in meditation you may find that your thoughts have gotten carried away, full of falsehoods and unreasonably alarmist. Meditation can help you determine which threats are real and which are exaggerations of your mind. Then you can let the offending thoughts go and feel the anxiety dissipate.

All cultures and religions have an ancient tradition of meditation. Some focus more on silent practice than others, but the basic method in all of them is shared. Most of these practices have seen a revival in recent years. They're especially appropriate in a time of crisis.

So how do you do it?

Some sit cross-legged on a cushion on the floor. This does provide a stable, supportive base and opens up the body for natural, unforced breath, but it is not necessary. Sitting on a chair, if more comfortable, can also provide a stable base for practice. Just sit forward on the seat, rest your feet firmly on the floor, and position your spine erect, shoulders back, chin tucked, head gently pressing up toward the ceiling. If you can, without discomfort, hold this position without support from the back of the chair.

If even that is uncomfortable, lean back or even lie down. The point is to be dignified and still, and to breathe naturally.

What to do with your hands can be a special distraction, so just fold them gently in your lap or place the palms down on your thighs.

In this position, focus on the breath. Breathe naturally through the nose, unless it's clogged, and focus on the rising and falling of your belly or the cooling sensation in the tip of your nostrils during each inhale, and the warming on each exhale. Counting breaths can help keep the focus on the breath, so count each breath, up to ten. Then begin again at one.

Other tips include closing your eyes to increase your focus on the breath. Or letting your eyes remain open while you drop your gaze to a spot a few feet in front of you and hold the gaze in soft focus to reduce blinking. Just remember, we're not taking a nap. We're falling awake.

Gently close your mouth, teeth slightly apart, and position your tongue behind your top teeth to reduce swallowing.

Focus on the breath, feeling the rise and fall of the belly, the subtle expansion and contraction of your chest and back, keeping the breath natural, not forcing it or trying to slow it down or breathe deeply. This is a practice to experience the present moment and although it may relax you, it is not a relaxation exercise. So keep everything just as it is, and return to the breath.

Thoughts will tumble through your mind and constantly pull your attention away from the breath. The mind will wander all over the place, and even after years of practice, thoughts will continue to interrupt. Just notice that you are thinking, let the thought go, and return the attention again to the breath. Don't chase each thought and don't start an internal conversation. Just dismiss the thought and come back to the breath, your point of focus, and count.

If you've lost your count at three or four, or find yourself at fifteen or twenty-seven when you meant to stop at ten, just let it go and begin again at one.

You'll find yourself constantly distracted by your thoughts. Notice that, and without judging yourself for being a poor meditator, return to the breath. Over and over.

Losing the count happens to everyone. In a way, since you keep losing your place and thoughts keep pulling you away from your count, meditation becomes an exercise in failure. Stick with it. Notice the failure. To notice is the whole point.

Discomfort is another challenge. If you find an itch, don't scratch it. Just focus the attention into that spot and experience the itch. If you feel bearable pain in your shoulder, or legs, or anywhere, do not reposition. Just direct the attention to that part of the body and focus on release with each exhale. Hold your position, focus on the breath, and experience your body in full. If you find a position becomes too painful, then respect the body and make adjustments as necessary.

Be kind to yourself and don't be overly ambitious. In the beginning, you may only be able to hold this attention for a few moments. The thoughts may become too much or the body too uncomfortable. Although today I meditate for thirty minutes each day, I began at only five, and it took a long time to work up from there. Just be aware that any period of focused attention is valuable, and persevere.

That's it. You don't need apps or books or expensive courses, although a good teacher can help if you hit a difficult patch of thoughts. Just do it every day and the benefits will accrue to you.

Meditation is as simple as breathing, and as natural. And while it has been challenging at times, over the years nothing has helped me manage my anxiety and bipolar disorder better.

Notice What is Happening in and Around You

Many people use meditation for relaxation or stress management or to foster an attitude of nonjudgment. It can do all of those things, but I like to think of meditation as a simple, focused way to notice what is going on, both within and around you. We're often distracted, especially when anxiety settles in, and we lose our ability to objectively observe what is real and what is not. In confronting anxiety we have to know the difference.

I've alluded to the fact that many of the thoughts we think are actually false. We exaggerate threats and worry about things that may never happen. This is what our brains are designed to do. It's an important survival mechanism that keeps us ever alert and keeps us ready for action. It's a catalyst for the fight or flight mechanism we looked at earlier. And like the physiological fight or flight response, this tendency to overemphasize threats helped our ancestors survive. It can do the same for us today, but much of the time it just screws us up.

Our thoughts often drag the past into the present or leave us fretting about the future. Thoughts about the past, which may be pleasant memories, may also be filled with regret about things we've done or replays of long past events during which we review what we may have done differently. Thoughts about the future may involve sensible, workable plans and ideas that spark creativity. But often they're worries about what might happen and unreasonable fears of things we don't have enough information about to be legitimately afraid of. These are the thoughts that spark anxiety, and when anxiety is aflame these thoughts just get more unnerving and more untrue.

This is where the ability to notice things through meditation can really help you. Of course, you notice the things around you and your body's experience of the world. That is foundational to any meditation practice. But as you focus on your breath and you are distracted by thoughts, you notice each one as it rises up. While you don't want to spend a lot of time on each thought, you may want to label them.

Identify each thought as a plan, or a worry, or a regret, or a fear. Notice which are negative and which are about joy. In a state of anxiety, inquire of each thought, "what is this about", and "is this true". Then put the thoughts away. Return to the breath.

Some of the most difficult, challenging thoughts will continue to pop up. Anxiety will constantly replay the fears, uncertainties and negations that fire it up. Make a mental note of this and be honest with yourself as you inquire about the truth of each thought. You'll probably find that many of the thoughts are patently untrue, and many others are exaggerations that really stretch the truth. In anxiety, you'll find that much of what you think, in fact, isn't true at all.

Meditation can give you the power to expose the lies and exaggerations your mind deals you, and the space to reassess them and consider them false. If you can do that you can set aside much of what makes anxiety unbearable and heal. Your mind can come to ease and your physical symptoms may get better or even cease. All this good can come from merely realizing the truth and being honest about the falsehoods that underpin your anxiety.

If, in meditation, you can take these steps successfully, you should practice daily, whether you feel anxiety coming on or not. It will benefit your mental health and make available an early warning system for when troubling emotions stalk you.

If you have an anxiety disorder you probably have a plan of medicine and therapy that you use when anxiety is present. The early warning system of body awareness and meditation will provide you the opportunity to implement such a plan before anxiety becomes disabling.

If you don't have a diagnosed anxiety disorder, anxiety in a time of crisis can still be disabling and lead to poor decisions. Even you can heed this early warning of impending anxiety and adjust your behavior to approach your situation, and the fear and uncertainty it brings, in a healthy way. Also, you can adjust your thoughts to stop the inaccuracies that will only make your anxiety worse.

All of this is available to the meditator. Sitting quietly with good posture focusing intently on your breath can do all of this for you. Focused attention exercises like the ones detailed in this book can expose, and even defeat, episodes of extreme anxiety. For a moment, though, I'd like to re-emphasize the practices of movement and standing, because classic, seated meditation is not for everyone.

Meditation is not Always the Answer

First of all, if you're in therapy, especially if you're in therapy for an anxiety disorder, don't think that meditation is going to eliminate the need for, or replace, that therapy. It can enhance it, but check with your therapist before you begin a practice.

If you take medicine for anxiety, or any other condition for that matter, don't even think that meditation will enable you to come off your medicine. Research has shown that meditation can be beneficial to almost every physical and mental health condition. It works great as an adjunct, or secondary, therapy. But please, only stop your meds if your doctor tells you to.

A period of high anxiety may not be the best time to begin a new meditation practice. It will work for many, so it's worth a try. If it's challenging, keep at it. Insightful realizations will come. But if you find yourself just sitting ruminating on, or going over and over without the ability to release them, negative thoughts, stay with exercise, healthy living, and productive and creative activity as your coping practices.

If you're captive to ceaseless negative rumination, beginning a meditation practice from scratch during a time of crisis could be like pouring gasoline onto a fire. Thoughts that experienced and some beginning meditators can identify as false may trip up others. As I've stated, meditation can help one notice their erroneous preconceptions and realize that the big errors they make come from following misleading thoughts about themselves and their conditions. Meditation can reveal that such anxiety producing thoughts are absolutely false. But the same meditation techniques in the hands of a ruminating beginner can make a mind that is spiraling from anxiety spin completely out of control.

People think meditation is supposed to calm them down and relax them. But all meditation really does is present to you your present experience, in the body and in the mind, exactly as it happens. If you feel good, so will meditation. But if you feel terrible, meditation is going to make you confront that and feel those emotions in all their terror. Yes, through meditation you can learn that the terror is often a creation of your internal dialogue, not the true world around you. The thoughts that keep you up at night or make you fearful of the present often have no basis in reality. After all, your thoughts are just that, thoughts. They may be full of doubt, anger, judgment or fear. They may have nothing to do with what is really going on in your life or your family's life. But when anxiety emerges they feel oh, so real. If you can let these thoughts go during meditation, great. But if you can't you're going to have to seek other ways to help you cope with anxiety. Like the other methods presented in this book.

Whether you meditate or not, finding and fostering community is one of the key means to cope. This can be a community of people who practice meditation together. These can be found online. At first it may seem silly to sit on a video conference with a lot of people not speaking, just sitting in silent focus, interacting only with their personal experience. But practicing with a group can strengthen your own practice. This, as with all forms of positive community, can be very supportive.

Online or app-based guided meditation, especially ones called body-scans, can help. But be sure you spend some time in silence with your own experience, rather than some guide's affirmations or ideas. To handle anxiety, you need to explore your body and your thoughts uninterrupted. Meditation can prepare you to accurately notice the effects of things that happen to you and influence your life. It can expose you to the full experience of your body and mind, how they are related, and how feelings in your body reflect the experience you have of your own thoughts.

Meditation can draw a baseline of truth for you about your situation and your physical and mental responses to it. Understanding the doubt that sometimes comes up during meditation can lead to better decisions. This is especially important because anxiety often freezes us into a state of indecision where nothing happens and nothing improves. In fact, in a state of anxiety things tend to get worse.

From the place of balance and reality you can find during meditation things appear to, and do, get better. You can identify the body's signals and set aside unhelpful thoughts and emotions and confront your anxiety from a place of truth. Combining truth and the strength that resides within you revealed during meditation are significant steps to take. These steps are crucial to positively and successfully meet and handle your anxiety.

Key Takeaways
- Meditation is a simple practice that can be done daily
- Meditation can reveal the thoughts that drive anxiety
- It is a great way to notice what is and what is not true in those thoughts
- Don't meditate if it leads to dangerous rumination

Chapter Five

Community in a Time of Crisis

I swear the dogs sense it too. They crowd the pillows and cower on the bed. They have had accidents in the house and are skittish on the leash. One has always been by our side, but now even the aloof one is clinging. She's curled up under the desk on my feet as I write. The most telling indicator of the energy in the house, in yourself, may be how your pets act. Right now things are nerve wracking. The pets, and the people, are all on edge. But at least we have them, and each other. To pet each beast and hold each other in unconditional love is soothing and bolsters any sense of security and safety. It's no wonder that right now, in many cities, the shelters are empty. The lost pets have found homes. They're finally needed.

We are social beings. We want to be around others. Some of us want more, or less, people in our lives, but there are always people in our lives. And like the pets that get us out of the house to walk past locked parks and garbage strewn gutters, around rubber gloves scattered on the sidewalk, we need the people jogging by, moving to the other side of the sidewalk and refusing eye contact. We need to reach out and cope.

Anxiety can make us feel achingly alone. When we're trapped in a panic believing that things have slipped out of control, we seek to join people. Either people who have the same fear or people who have a confident sense of direction, pointing the way out. But when we're made suspicious of each other's bodies and told to keep six feet apart it's hard to join together and resolve a difficult situation. We've always been assured that there is safety in numbers. But now even a crowd of like-minded people has become a threat, and we're left increasingly alone to deal with the stress that sickens us in ways that can be just as negative to our healing as the illness caused by the virus.

We were retreating into competing camps suspicious of strangers before the contagion emerged. Political issues, class issues, and racial issues conspired to pull us apart. But in our families, with our friends, sometimes at work, even on our block in the city, we tolerated each other's differences and stayed together, frayed, most of the time. Then co-workers in the breakroom, patrons down the bar, and parents on the playground by the swing-set all became suspect. We each pop our trunks at the grocery store and a faceless clerk, deemed essential, drops in the bags and closes the boot. We drive away with no opportunity to even say hello.

Church has always been a community of comfort, a ritual of sameness to set the week and feel included, but even that experience has changed. First they stopped offering the cup at communion. The next week we couldn't shake hands while passing the peace. Then the church closed, as did all the shops and bakeries, the dry cleaners and the coffee shops, and we sit on the couch on Sunday morning, thumbnails in the margin, while the pastor freezes on the screen due to a poor connection. Even the broadband has petered out.

We lean on others to help us cope. We find new ways to be a community. My daughter has started a spy club with her friends on Messenger. Recently, on a sun-kissed spring afternoon, as the trees began to bud and blossom, the neighbors drifted out onto their stoops and my daughter drew skewed chalk circles, six feet apart, in the street. People still stand in them and talk, drinking the last of the wine or the cheap bourbon from the back of the cabinet. An infant across the street had his first birthday. His parents rolled his stroller in front of the house and we stood at our distance and sang Happy Birthday. Nothing like this has ever happened before.

As we try to hold together a semblance of society beyond the walls of our homes, we can find ourselves in anxiety provoking encounters that just weeks before wouldn't have warranted a second thought. Merely buying groceries is suddenly fraught with challenges. Items are out of stock and what we do buy needs to be wiped down with anti-bacterial wipes as soon as we take them out of the bags in the kitchen. Then there's the flash of surprise as you realize you've touched your face. We seem like beginners in everything we do. No longer can we just go through the motions, for every motion has unforeseen consequences. Rote actions seem brand new.

In newness things seem fresh, and there is goodness to discover. Community remains and in it we cope. Building new connections is the best way to cope in a crisis. If the mindset you're familiar with becomes threatening, you can build a new one and include the people that help. Leave behind no one you can reach, and no one who reaches you. You'll need them, and they'll need you.

There's so much technology and media we can call on to maintain and make new connections. A friend who teaches guitar has kept most of his students. He gives lessons on FaceTime. My neighbor takes a Spanish class with a group on Zoom. Lectures from the world's greatest professors at the world's most esteemed universities are up for free online. Exercise classes from famous trainers are streamed all day. The groups a person can join have exploded in capacity and opportunity as the restrictions of space and place disappear. The denizens of social media made promises of unbound potential for community for years. That promise is finally coming true.

Even acts that keep us focused on ourselves as individuals can open us up to include the world.

Practices in focused attention like walking, standing and seated meditation work best when we save some of the focus we direct for others. The helpless loneliness that exacerbates anxiety can become comfort when we join a circle. Even online. We are the witness to each other's suffering. We are the salve for each other's wounds. We realize we must continue on together.

It will be tough. Anxiety will trap you inside yourself and make you feel worthless or dangerously inconsistent. You'll be afraid to reach out. You may fear being hurt even more than you fear confronting one more day with this irritable, trembling, negative energy. But in a crisis almost everyone is fearing that. We can best cope in a crisis, we can best soothe our agitated minds, by making connections. As the methods in this book give you some secure space to act, reach out to others. Help them. They need you. Ask for help. You need them.

There's a type of anxiety that grates on me. It's found in the person who sits and contemplates the world's problems before their own. They identify with some possible solution and sit idle instructing everyone else on how bad things are and what needs to be done. All the while doing nothing. Right now people curse government inaction for not providing enough ventilators or masks, or closing beaches too late, or testing only the advantaged, leaving those impoverished to suffer undiagnosed and untreated. These people sit smug that they know better and have figured out what could have been, what should have been, different. Yet they do nothing but fend for themselves. They're left cut off to handle their own anxiety, and they suffer more from the inward focus that only looks out to criticize and complain.

A crisis is a time to come together without complaint. We must realize that the things that divide us are much smaller than the common cause that in a crisis unites us. We should be cautious and not allow differences like political leanings to distract us from working together in community. In a crisis, too much political involvement can be disruptive. Together we need to address both our shared humanity and real workable solutions. While we can remain vigilant for factions that may attempt to use a crisis for a power grab, we must above all embrace the community we share in good times and, especially, in troubled times.

You can soothe your anxiety by jumping in and helping. In the Covid-19 crisis you can't just show up at an emergency room and volunteer, and many shelters, petri dishes for the spreading pathogen, have closed. But small action still helps. Find the GoFundMe page for that coffee shop you used to stop at every morning. Knock on an elderly neighbor's door just to check on them and see if they need anything. Call your niece or your great-aunt. Put an employee who doesn't really have to be on the conference call on the call so she doesn't feel so trapped and alone, working at home, disconnected, unsure of her purpose. Make eye contact with that person jogging by and say hello from a safe distance.

When in a well-spaced line outside a grocery store, walk back to the older man struggling with his endurance standing several people behind you and offer to trade places. Join the virtual sewing club that makes masks for the local hospital and learn to sew. These are small gestures, to be sure. Small gestures forge a community and enlarge each of us enough to overcome the task at hand; the challenge we refuse to allow to set us back.

With calm and grace we can take gentle steps to help each other cope with the uncertainty and anxiety of a larger crisis that alone seems too big to comprehend and too complicated to impact. Yet we can understand each other and positively impact a world in disarray one small act at a time.

Sartre wrote "Hell is other people." The line is misquoted and misunderstood. The way people toss it around is wrong. After you've spent time focused inward identifying and handling your personal anxiety, realize that full recovery from anxiety continues with your interactions with other people. In other people we can find hell, if anxiety causes us to distort our vision, and our connection to community. Coping with anxiety is an inclusive practice. Hope is other people.

To maintain that hope you have to stay connected. If you live alone, this is crucial. Reach out to family, friends, co-workers or people you meet online. Even if you're at home with a large family, remaining in touch with the life you had with friends, clubs and activities outside the house is important. However, this must be done with respect to stay at home orders and social distancing. Most of it is going to have to be done virtually.

My friend John and I have had coffee every Thursday for years. It is an intellectual feast and I treasure that time. We still get together, on FaceTime. I'd meet my friend Scott for lunch once a week to discuss books, art and big ideas. Today we send each other writing samples, photos and excerpts as attachments to emails and call each other often. My extended family has game night on Sundays, completely online. My parents, siblings and their families are all on the screen, talking over each other, laughing. Just like when we get together.

An actual source of joy has been learning new technology. It's amazing what I've been taught by my nine-year-old, and in turn my wife and I have used that knowledge to bring my in-laws into the 21st century. They're alone in a house in an adult community and relish the chance to spend time in cyberspace with their granddaughter. My father-in-law's interests continue to expand. He said he was so bored he baked corn muffins. The man had never before cooked anything in his life. Once he got past the instructions to grease a pan, which he had no idea how to do, he was fine. The muffins, my mother-in-law said, came out delicious. We can all use this time to be students and teachers.

Remember, though, that quantity time beats quality time always. Short, daily drop-ins with family and friends, even if you have little to say, are crucial to keep relationships strong. Not knowing what's happening with others and feeling disconnected from people are significant sources of anxiety. You can correct that by just touching base. I'm in touch with my parents now more than I have been in years. We can't see each other face-to-face, but we feel close and supportive of each other. Sometimes to just reach out with a text that asks, "how are you?" can raise the spirits of both you and your contact enough.

As for kids, at least for the foreseeable future, the battle for screen time has been decided. They have won. Crafting and Friday night dance parties in the living room keep them engaged for a while, but we adults have things that need to get done. The screen helps. Just monitor it to make sure they are using their, and your, devices for learning and connecting with friends and family. No one gains anything if your child is mindlessly watching videos on how to make slime.

Once you have found a place of peace, strengthening connections and building community even in disturbing times can help us handle the uncertainty that contributes to anxiety. This outward focus is a great complement to all the inner work we can ever do.

Certainty can be found in a future that seals your fate with those you care about, those you aspire to be with, and those you depend on. If you're lost within yourself, turn to others. The world is in turmoil and we know nothing about how this will end and what will be left for us. Don't give up. Part of handling anxiety is looking outside, toward the future, as part of a group willing to search together. We must be sure to bring along the least of us.

Key Takeaways

- Community is necessary to resolve a crisis
- Reach out to others. Find like-minded people online
- Explore new interests with new groups
- Contact family and friends often

Chapter Six

The Path Within

Another part of handling anxiety and coping in a crisis is to find the path within.

The healthy condition of the mind that sanctions you to rise to the challenge of the crisis, to make beneficial choices and position yourself so you can thrive in the inevitable changes to come, can be drawn on from a place formed deep within you. To face a crisis like the one resulting from coronavirus is anxiety producing enough. To stare it down as an individual left to their own resources can be harrowing. But it must be done.

Anxiety fades in the light of supportive community. In this age of social isolation composure inside of you can also be found. Practice the therapies in this book. Don't attach to your anxiety. While this situation is full blown bad, you've probably felt something anxiety provoking before. You're prepared for this.

Don't attach to your anxiety. In a troubled time we cling to what is familiar, like a child hugs the stuffed animal she sleeps with. In a safe and healthy situation this thing, person or thought we cling to is loving and comforting. But in a bad situation, when all we know and all we feel is anxiety, we may latch onto the terror. It may be all we know. At the worst of a crisis it may be all we have left, and we're desperate to not let that go too. Then we will have lost everything.

It's not uncommon in a world of dimming possibilities to identify with the threat. To surrender to the idea that you're merely controlled by something which has taken hold of you and now forces you into a state of reaction. In this state you may succumb to the fear that everything is out of control and we are acted upon by something bigger than each of us. Something that is out to get us. But a virus does not make choices and does not target you. It is completely without malice as it spreads. We must be careful not to give it animate form. We must not allow our minds to create an enemy that has us in its crosshairs.

A virus, like a storm or a shattered economy, just is. We shouldn't give it the power of personality. We have the wits to carefully respond to it and make the risk to ourselves less likely. We can stay home most of the time and when out keep a safe distance and wear a mask. We have the will to recover from any setbacks. We have the capacity to change our situation and moderate things that threaten us. We have science and finance and infrastructure. The virus has nothing but itself.

It is insidious, but it has no will of its own. Of course it's bad. We don't just make it so in our minds. Right now it seems to decide our fate for us. Yet it doesn't.

Crisis offers us an opportunity to reshape ourselves and our place in the world.

Freedom from anxiety requires us to let go of the negative we cling to. The false ideas and unfounded fears to which we're attached. Your body signals that you're ill and your thoughts hang the hooks that hold the chains that entrap you in a state of internal crisis. All around you may be seen as falling apart. But you don't have to.

I return to the quote from James Baldwin that leads off this book: "I would like to think of myself as being able to face whatever it is I have to face as me..." The quote goes on: "... without having my identity dependent on something that finally has to be believed."[2]

When we experience anxiety in a time of crisis, we have to come to terms with what is true. Belief is important. For some, as faith, it's foundational. It helps to believe that things will get better, and it helps to believe that with all the turmoil in the world the crisis will not destroy us. A belief like this is easy to hold and lean on because it's probably true. In the big world with its massive numbers of people the majority of us, health wise at least, will come out of this OK.

Belief also underlies anxiety. We wouldn't suffer from anxiety if at some level we didn't believe that the worst is yet to come, and it will directly involve us. Belief is a two-edged sword, and to get beyond a crisis we'll likely have to let it go. As Peter Viereck said: "Reality is that which, when you don't believe it, doesn't go away."[3]

That leaves us only with what is. That is all the information we need to navigate a crisis as large as the one that currently challenges our health, our security, and our way of life.

Some approximations are necessary. The math of epidemiology relies on probability, probability relies on confidence intervals, and confidence intervals help us project most likely scenarios. The math is solid. It doesn't depend on belief.

Uncertainty and Belief

In order for society to survive we're going to have to set aside ideology and preconceptions and adhere to facts and assured projections. To get through this as individuals, we're going to have to suspend belief and work with what we know for sure. Severe anxiety depends on belief. It relies on us not being able to relate to the data. It elevates things that aren't presently true, often things we know aren't presently true, and seals them into our searching minds as undisputed fact. Only a few facts support it. The crisis may envelope you. It may ruin your life financially. It may take your loved ones. But in all likelihood, for many of us, right now it hasn't, and we're likely exaggerating the threat, even if the threat is huge. Severe anxiety, dysfunctional anxiety, requires that you overestimate threats and underestimate your capacity to face them.

Belief is hard to snap out of. Throughout your life you may have attributed so many good things to things you believe in. In anxiety, you believe something bad will happen. Either way, good or bad, belief has little to do with what actually happens to you. You must face each challenge on its own merits, armed only with reason and good information, without the anxiety inducing stranglehold of belief.

Belief is a challenge. It makes up much of our self-identity. We must let go of our beliefs in order to achieve a secure idea of who we are and what we face. This is odd, because so much of what we think we know, and much of what we expect, is tied up in belief rather than facts. A crisis gives us a tremendous opportunity to investigate this dilemma and discover how who we are sometimes contradicts who we think we are.

This contradiction is often supported only by anxiety.

This idea of belief does not speak to faith. Belief is the acceptance that a statement is true or that something exists. Faith is complete trust or confidence in someone or something. Belief requires a choice. Faith is the willing suspension of disbelief that transcends uncertainty. Belief can fail you.

In a crisis the questioned security of a job that is suddenly lost to a whim of profitability or the severity of the economic downturn erodes the belief in a system that for most of us serves us well. The ties of family necessary to sustain us falter when a spouse is not even allowed into the intensive care unit to sit with a partner on a ventilator who may not make it through the night. Even funerals are prohibited. So many beliefs are sacrificed to uncertainty. Security about the future erodes as beliefs we hold without question are no longer supported by society's efforts to manage, and eventually defeat, the pandemic.

For many of us, our sense of self resides firmly in a collection of beliefs. Anxiety resides at the intersection of uncertainty and belief. When the vehicle of the self meets the weight of the crisis, this is the intersection where they collide.

A Response to Crisis

I know a woman who has run right into the conflict of uncertainty and belief that the crisis has forced on her. She is a tremendous success in business but comes from a very poor background. Her identity is intimately tied up in her story about this achievement. She was the first in her family to go to college and bought her first house as a single woman. Her old-world family expects women to get married and have children, not careers, so her rise in business not only defines her, it sets her apart. She believes she has overcome expectations and blazed a trail for others.

Another belief she holds, the story she tells herself when things are very quiet, quiet enough to entertain doubt, is that if she stops moving up in her career she will end up back in poverty. She believes she must forge onward, even to the detriment of her health, to be able to support her family. She has saved a ton of money. She has demonstrated marketable skills. There is no way that if her career were interrupted she would end up destitute. Yet even though this story doesn't stand up to reason, she believes it. It, too, defines her.

The uncertainty of the present crisis and its impact on the business for which she works means that layoffs are imminent. She may soon be without work. She's a valuable employee with great responsibility, but who knows? Uncertainty exposes and assaults her belief that she is one failure away from ruin. Terrible anxiety is the result.

In a case like this, anxiety feeds on itself. She works harder. She puts in longer hours. Even though because of the stay at home order she now works from home, sometimes her only contact with her family for hours is when she yells "Shut up!" down the hall. She's afraid that if the sounds of children playing or arguing are heard in the background of a conference call other attendees on the call will take her less seriously. They might think she's not giving her all. Uncertainty and belief have led her away from the bonding experience some families are having in the crisis. She's not sitting down for family dinners. She's not exploring new interests with her children. She keeps putting off hobbies she set aside for years, even though this would be a perfect time to pursue them. She's not contacting old friends on social media. Her belief meets uncertainty and she only works harder, ever afraid. Her belief has claws in her now that uncertainty has exposed it. Her anxiety levels are too extreme for anyone to survive for long without breaking.

Even this deep into uncertainty my friend believes she can still direct what happens in her life. She fears the crisis will wrestle control from her. This hardens her belief that if she loses control she will end up back in poverty. None of this is true, but her identity clings to it and anxiety worsens as her sense of self breaks.

What lies at the core of her problem is that her sense of self is entirely wrapped up in beliefs instead of a rational investigation of her present circumstances. As we explored in the chapter on meditation, she is dragging the past into the present and pushing the doubts and fears she encounters into the future. Of course, the future is uncertain.

It would help her to examine her beliefs as they influence her behavior in these unforeseen circumstances. It would help her to explore some of the techniques outlined in this book. In meditation she could inventory her beliefs and label each one positive or negative. That could reveal which beliefs are true and which ones are patently false. She may realize that she is in a much better place than she believes she is. If she still gets no relief, she should talk to someone neutral. Someone who will ask questions and just listen without judgment. Someone she feels does not have a vested interest in her success or failure. Plenty of opportunities for this sort of conversation are available today through employee assistance programs or teletherapy providers.

Anxiety can be an Opportunity

If we return to the idea of probable outcomes, if we compare beliefs we hold about ourselves with the most likely outcomes instead of the tragedies we envision, we can begin to free ourselves from disabling anxiety. As stated at the very beginning of this book, anxiety is normal. As we face the future, especially in a time of crisis, moderate anxiety is warranted. If we practice daily, if we actively work with discipline to reduce anxiety, we can keep it from becoming unreasonable. We can keep it from crippling us and making us sick. In a crisis we must approach uncertainty with caution, but we must not let that caution overwhelm us.

Anxiety founded on things you actually know, or things that trusted sources inform you of, is normal and protective. It helps you make good decisions, survive and thrive. So, when informed and rational people tell us we should practice social isolation we must. No matter what we believe. Protective anxiety demands it. But when anxiety explodes into illness it's surely dependent on those things you know turning into conjecture. We extrapolate worst-case scenarios. This can lead to poor decisions and withdrawal from the world. The irony is that there, where terrible anxiety forces us to go to protect ourselves, we are not safe. Anxiety then no longer protects us, it damages us.

Try this exercise: Take out a piece of paper and write down your thoughts as you consider the crisis that contributes to the uncertainty about the future which drives your anxiety. What do you know for sure? What do you project to be your best-case and worst-case scenarios? What facts support them?

List your broad, determining beliefs, the big things about life, culture and place. The things that drive you or hold you back. Then boil this list down to specific beliefs about yourself. Beliefs that consider your skills, possibilities and the support you have in your life. Contemplate this list for a while. Sleep on it.

Reconsider your list. On another piece of paper collect the beliefs that persist. Include fears of outcomes that are unclear. Include exaggerations. Be honest with yourself and include every belief that has no basis in reality. Your list can be long or it can be short. One or two beliefs may override all the others.

Meditate on how these beliefs influence your life. Is this influence positive or negative? Can you balance the uncertainty of the present situation with the most probable outcomes?

It's silly to say cross out the beliefs that really don't make sense and get over it. These beliefs, even if exposed as unfounded, still make up your sense of self. Just as in meditation when you investigate and expose your fallacies, you must also reconsider how your sense of self is influenced by the uncertainty of the crisis that collides with your beliefs.

Beliefs are exceptionally difficult to free yourself from. Look back at your list. This time consider the facts alone – what you know in fact to be true. In those facts you can begin to liberate yourself from the prison of belief. And anxiety.

Each of us is going to have to face the facts with confidence, creativity and reliable information, as well as the love and support of our families and friends, and act accordingly.

As you contemplate your situation consider the causes of anxiety that are presented to you only by belief or by quiet, repeated, ill-conceived stories that reinforce those beliefs. In order to face whatever it is you have to face — shortages, job loss, illness — you'll have to suspend the conclusions you jump to and rewrite your life. Avoid the terror that lies behind unfounded belief.

Belief is challenging, yet it makes up much of our definition of self. A crisis gives us a tremendous opportunity to investigate this and discover how who we are sometimes contradicts who we think we are. Anxiety, for all its ills, gives us that chance.

It's OK to have anxiety. You can cope with that. But you must not become it. Don't identify with the terror and uncertainty you feel inside. It's not you, and I hope I've convinced you that most of the time your fears are often about things you've fabricated. Your body and mind have conspired to make you ill. Your body and mind can work together to make you well again.

Try not to listen to people who say, "Get over it." You can't.

But you can handle it. You can cope with it. Anxiety may get a piece of you, but it doesn't have to get the better of you.

You'll never be free of anxiety. In reasonable amounts anxiety is a good thing. It is protective and thought provoking. To free yourself of unfounded, damaging anxiety, free yourself from the uncertainty that in a crisis confines you. Handling anxiety in a time of crisis is a skill you can develop.

A time of crisis strips our lives down to what is truly important and what is truly ours. That may be the silver lining.

Too much anxiety can cheat you of this chance to rediscover and reset your life. Get real. The crisis sure is. In that reality you'll find the reserves that enable you to be equal to the task, to love yourself and others, and to find a reason to go on in peace. You'll find the sense to make the decisions that can bring you successfully through the challenges you face.

Anxiety doesn't have to be a disability. Anxiety can be an opportunity.

Key Takeaways

- Don't attach to anxiety. Don't identify with the threat of the crisis
- Discover beliefs about yourself and your life
- Contemplate how uncertainty impacts these beliefs and causes anxiety
- Use the opportunity provided by the crisis to grow

Afterword

They say a doctor never takes his own medicine, but as I wrote this book I sure had to take mine.

As I turn in this manuscript we have been in quarantine, or lock down, or shelter in place, or under a stay at home order for 28 days. Our publisher, Tim Ward at Changemakers Books, gave each of us authors of the Resilience Series a daunting task: write a book that can truly help people, a book for people suffering in a time of crisis, in three weeks. We are rushing to press work we hope will be immediately beneficial for people with immediate, pressing problems. And work that will last for people facing crises in the future.

I turn in a book about anxiety written from a place of high anxiety. Social isolation is nothing new for a writer. It's what we do. It's how we work. But there are people in my space now all day long, and the dogs bark to get out and run.

I usually write slowly, but not now. I've been getting up two hours early and staying up two hours later than everyone else, taking precious time to work. When my wife is done with her work I say, "Tag, you're it" and run upstairs to knock out some more. She and I are in the same space for 24 hours a day and we have spent absolutely no time together. We're struggling to get some special quality time with our daughter. We try to teach her. We hope that from this she learns about community, responsibility, self-sacrifice and how to manage boredom. We hope that somehow she'll be better off for all of this.

We're inordinately busy. Our friends and family share this experience. I have no idea who these people are who binge watch Netflix and clean out the basement during this time. I know none of them.

I catch myself trembling and questioning everything. The groceries come three days late and half the items we order are missing. Yesterday the CDC recommended that people wear masks when out in public. The rod that holds the shower curtain broke, so I have to go to the hardware store to buy a new one. I'm actually a little scared. My uncle is in the intensive care unit with the virus. My aunt and cousin are home in bed with fevers. Our investment portfolio is decimated. We are among the lucky ones.

Last week, carrying something down the stairs, I twisted my leg and heard a pop! like a gunshot. I could barely walk. No doctors were taking appointments, and I'm not sure I would feel safe walking into a medical office or urgent care right now anyway. On telehealth a physical therapist who thinks I've torn my meniscus gave me some exercises and the knee has gotten better. But it still hurts to walk the dogs and I'm taking the stairs one at a time. I don't know when a doctor will be able to look at it.

Through this I let things go wrong for a little while. I didn't meditate for a few days, I stopped eating, and drank so much coffee it feels like I burned a hole in my esophagus. I looked at a blank page and tried to write. It was rubbish.

I had let anxiety seep into me and I fell hard into it.

Finally, I returned to the practices I've written about in this book and I settled down. The anxiety, normal in the face of all this, eased just enough to get by. It has eased some more since.

I know the methods in this book work because I've been practicing them for years. All of this practice has been gearing me up for right now. If I didn't have this experience handling anxiety, I would have come completely apart days ago. I'd sit huddled in the corner, terrified, an empty notebook on the desk.

I hope you try what's in this book, and I honestly and sincerely hope it helps. I believe it will. Right now we have no idea when this will peak. We have no idea when we'll feel safe away from home, no idea when the office and school will re-open, no idea if we'll sit in the stadium and cheer at a baseball game this summer. Today, as I turn in this manuscript, there are no answers.

Of course, this will change. We'll go to church again, see our parents in person, and drink at the pub on the corner. We'll get over our anxiety. Until then, I'll adhere to my own advice and follow the guidelines I've offered here. A crisis will come again, maybe not one as destructive as this one, but a crisis, nonetheless. Right now, it feels anxiety has always been our common experience, and always is our common experience. But it hasn't been and it is not. Yet when fully in the grip of anxiety, it's all you know. But by knowing that, by approaching anxiety with learned, proven techniques, you can handle it.

Stay positive, stay productive, and stay peaceful. Be safe. Be there for others. You can learn a lot about yourself in a crisis. You can grow. I turn in this manuscript and return to handling the anxiety of everyday life. Bless you. Be strong. Human will enables healing, and life remains vital still. It may be different, but we'll thrive, with the courage to engage the future again.

About the Author

After a series of hospitalizations and a lot of bad behavior, George Hofmann managed to overcome the worst of bipolar disorder by adding practices in focused attention to the usual therapies of medicine and talk. He works to show others with anxiety, depression and bipolar disorder how to do the same. He maintains the site "Practicing Mental Illness", which promotes meditation, movement and meaningful work as keys to growth and healing. George has conducted workshops on meditation for individuals, families, support groups, healthcare professionals and corporations. He lives in Philadelphia, Pennsylvania with his wife, their daughter and two poorly behaved dogs. His upcoming book, *Practicing Mental Illness* ISBN 978-1-78904-626-7 will be published by Changemakers Books in 2021.

www.practicingmentalillness.com

Endnotes

1. The Pro-Truth Pledge is an initiative promoting truth seeking and rational thinking, particularly in politics. www.protruthpledge.org

2. Baldwin, J, McCummings, L, X, Malcolm, "Black Muslims vs. the Sit-ins," WBAI, April 25, 1961, pacificradioarchives.org/recording/bb5322

3. Viereck, P. 1997, *Clio is no Cleo: The messiness of history.* Lecture, *Soc* **41**, 10–14, Mt Holyoke College

TRANSFORMATION

The *Resilience* Series

The Resilience Series is a collaborative effort by the authors of Changemakers Books in response to the 2020 coronavirus epidemic. Each concise volume offers expert advice and practical exercises for mastering specific skills and abilities. Our intention is that by strengthening your resilience, you can better survive and even thrive in a time of crisis.

Resilience: Adapt and Plan for the New Abnormal of the COVID-19 Coronavirus Pandemic
by Gleb Tsipursky

COVID-19 has demonstrated clearly that businesses, nonprofits, individuals, and governments are terrible at dealing effectively with large-scale disasters that take the form of slow-moving trainwrecks. Using cutting-edge research in cognitive neuroscience and behavioral economics on dangerous judgment errors (cognitive biases), this book first explains why we respond so poorly to slow-moving, high-impact, and long-term crises. Next, the book shares research-based strategies for how organizations and individuals can adapt effectively to the new abnormal of the COVID-19 pandemic and similar disasters. Finally, it shows how to develop an effective strategic plan and make the best major decisions in the context of the uncertainty and ambiguity brought about by COVID-19 and other slow-moving large-scale catastrophes. The author, a cognitive neuroscientist and behavioral economist and CEO of the consulting, coaching, and training firm Disaster Avoidance Experts, combines research-based strategies with real-life stories from his business and nonprofit clients as they adapt to the pandemic.

Resilience: Aging with Vision, Hope and Courage in a Time of Crisis
by John C. Robinson

This book is for those over 65 wrestling with fear, despair, insecurity, and loneliness in these frightening times. A blend of psychology, self-help, and spirituality, it's meant for all who hunger for facts, respect, compassion, and meaningful resources to light their path ahead. The 74-year-old author's goal is to move readers from fear and paralysis to growth and engagement: "Acknowledging the inspiring resilience and wisdom of our hard-won maturity, I invite you on a personal journey of transformation and renewal into a new consciousness and a new world."

Resilience: Connecting with Nature in a Time of Crisis
by Melanie Choukas-Bradley

Nature is one of the best medicines for difficult times. An intimate awareness of the natural world, even within the city, can calm anxieties and help create healthy perspectives. This book will inspire and guide you as you deal with the current crisis, or any personal or worldly distress. The author is a naturalist and certified forest therapy guide who leads nature and forest bathing walks for many organizations in Washington, DC and the American West. Learn from her the Japanese art of "forest bathing": how to tune in to the beauty and wonder around you with all your senses, even if your current sphere is a tree outside the window or a wild backyard. Discover how you can become a backyard naturalist, learning about the trees, wildflowers, birds and animals near your home. Nature immersion during stressful times can bring comfort and joy as well as opportunities for personal growth, expanded vision and transformation.

Resilience: Going Within in a Time of Crisis
by P.T. Mistlberger

During a time of crisis, we are presented with something of a fork in the road; we either look within and examine ourselves, or engage in distractions and go back to sleep. This book is intended to be a companion for men and women dedicated to their inner journey. Written by the author of seven books and founder of several personal growth communities and esoteric schools, each chapter offers different paths for exploring your spiritual frontier: advanced meditation techniques, shadow work, conscious relating, dream work, solo retreats, and more. In traversing these challenging times, let this book be your guide.

Resilience: Grow Stronger in a Time of Crisis
by Linda Ferguson

Many of us have wondered how we would respond in the midst of a crisis. You hope that difficult times could bring out the best in you. Some become stronger, more resilient and more innovative under pressure. You hope that you will too. But you are afraid that crisis may bring out your anxiety, your fears and your weakest communication. No one knows when the crisis will pass and things will get better. That's out of your hands. But *you* can get better. All it takes is an understanding of how human beings function at their best, the willpower to make small changes in perception and behavior, and a vision of a future that is better than today. In the pages of this book, you will learn to create the conditions that allow your best self to show up and make a difference – for you and for others.

Resilience: Handling Anxiety in a Time of Crisis
by George Hofmann

It's a challenging time for people who experience anxiety, and even people who usually don't experience it are finding their moods are getting the better of them. Anxiety hits hard and its symptoms are unmistakable, but sometimes in the rush and confusion of uncertainty we miss those symptoms until it's too late. When things seem to be coming undone, it's still possible to recognize the onset of anxiety and act to prevent the worst of it. The simple steps taught in this book can help you overcome the turmoil.

Resilience: The Life-Saving Skill of Story
by Michelle Auerbach

Storytelling covers every skill we need in a crisis. We need to share information about how to be safe, about how to live together, about what to do and not do. We need to talk about what is going on in ways that keep us from freaking out. We need to change our behavior as a human race to save each other and ourselves. We need to imagine a possible future different from the present and work on how to get there. And we need to do it all without falling apart. This book will help people in any field and any walk of life to become better storytellers and immediately unleash the power to teach, learn, change, soothe, and create community to activate ourselves and the people around us.

Resilience: Navigating Loss in a Time of Crisis
by Jules De Vitto

This book explores the many forms of loss that can happen in times of crisis. These losses can range from loss of business, financial security, routine, structure to the deeper losses of meaning, purpose or identity. The author draws on her background in transpersonal psychology, integrating spiritual insights and mindfulness practices to take the reader on a journey in which to help them navigate the stages of uncertainty that follow loss. The book provides several practical activities, guided visualization and meditations to cultivate greater resilience, courage and strength and also explores the potential to find greater meaning and purpose through times of crisis.

Resilience: Virtually Speaking
Communicating at a Distance
by Teresa Erickson and Tim Ward

To adapt to a world where you can't meet face-to-face – with air travel and conferences cancelled, teams working from home – leaders, experts, managers and professionals all need to master the skills of virtual communication. Written by the authors of *The Master Communicator's Handbook*, this book tells you how to create impact with your on-screen presence, use powerful language to motivate listening, and design compelling visuals. You will also learn techniques to prevent your audience from losing attention, to keep them engaged from start to finish, and to create a lasting impact.

Resilience: Virtual Teams
Holding the Center When You Can't Meet Face-to-Face
by Carlos Valdes-Dapena

In the face of the COVID-19 virus organizations large and small are shuttering offices and factories, requiring as much work as possible be done from people's homes. The book draws on the insights of the author's earlier book, *Lessons from Mars,* providing a set of the powerful tools and exercises developed within the

Mars Corporation to create high performance teams. These tools have been adapted for teams suddenly forced to work apart, in many cases for the first time. These simple secrets and tested techniques have been used by thousands of teams who know that creating a foundation of team identity and shared meaning makes them resilient, even in a time of crisis.